Farndon, John, 1960–

Volcanoes & earthquakes
and other facts about

BULLETPOINTS

VOLCANOES & EARTHQUAKES

AND OTHER FACTS ABOUT PLANET EARTH

John Farndon
Consultant: Peter Riley

Miles Kelly
PUBLISHING

First published by Miles Kelly Publishing Ltd
Bardfield Centre, Great Bardfield
Essex, CM7 4SL

Copyright © 2003 Miles Kelly Publishing
Some material in this book first appeared in *1000 Things You Should Know*

2 4 6 8 10 9 7 5 3 1

Editor
Isla MacCuish

Design
WhiteLight

Picture Research
Liberty Newton

Inputting
Carol Danenbergs

British Library Cataloguing-in-Publication Data
A catalogue record for this book is available from the British Library

ISBN 1-84236-238-0

Printed in China

www.mileskelly.net
info@mileskelly.net

The publishers would like to thank the following artists who have contributed to this book:

Gary Hincks, Janos Marffy, Guy Smith

Contents

Formation of the Earth

- **The Earth formed** 4.57 billion years ago out of debris left over from the explosion of a giant star.

- **The Earth began to form** as star debris spun round the newly formed Sun and clumped into rocks called planetesimals.

- **Planetesimals** were pulled together by their own gravity to form planets such as Earth and Mars.

- **At first** the Earth was a seething mass of molten rock.

- **After 50 million years** a giant rock cannoned into the newborn Earth. The impact melted the rock into a hot splash, which cooled to become our Moon.

- **The shock of the impact** that formed the Moon made iron and nickel collapse towards the Earth's centre. They formed a core so dense that its atoms fuse in nuclear reactions that have kept the inside of the Earth hot ever since.

- **The molten rock** formed a thick mantle about 3000 km thick around the metal core. The core's heat keeps the mantle warm and churning, like boiling porridge.

- **After about 100 million years** the surface of the mantle cooled and hardened to form a thin crust.

- **Steam and gases** billowing from volcanoes formed the Earth's first, poisonous atmosphere.

- **After 200 million years** the steam had condensed to water. It fell in huge rain showers to form the oceans.

▲ *When the Earth formed from a whirling cloud of stardust, the pieces rushed together with such force that the young planet turned into a fiery ball. It slowly cooled down, and the continents and oceans formed.*

5

The Ages of the Earth

- **The Earth formed 4570 million years ago (mya)** but the first animals with shells and bones appeared less than 600 mya. It is mainly with the help of their fossils that geologists have learned about the Earth's history since then. We know very little about the 4000 million years before, known as Precambrian Time.

- **Just as days are divided** into hours and minutes, so geologists divide the Earth's history into time periods. The longest are eons, thousands of millions of years long. The shortest are chrons, a few thousand years long. In between come eras, periods, epochs and ages.

- **The years since Precambrian Time** are split into three eras: Palaeozoic, Mesozoic and Cenozoic.

- **Different plants and animals** lived at different times, so geologists can tell from the fossils in rocks how long ago the rocks formed. Using fossils, they have divided the Earth's history since Precambrian Time into 11 periods.

2 mya

Quaternary Period: many mammals die out in Ice Ages; humans evolve

65 mya

Tertiary Period: first large mammals; birds flourish; widespread grasslands

144 mya

Cretaceous Period: first flowering plants; the dinosaurs die out

213 mya

Jurassic Period: dinosaurs widespread; Archaeopteryx, earliest known bird

248 mya

Triassic Period: first mammals; seed-bearing plants spread; Europe is in the tropics

286 mya

Permian Period: conifers replace ferns as big trees; deserts are widespread

- **Layers of rock** form on top of each other, so the oldest rocks are usually at the bottom and the youngest at the top, unless they have been disturbed. The order of layers from top to bottom is known as the geological column.

- **By looking for certain fossils** geologists can tell if one layer of rock is older than another.

- **Fossils can only show** if a rock is older or younger than another; they cannot give a date in years. Also, many rocks such as igneous rocks contain no fossils. To give an absolute date, geologists may use radiocarbon dating.

- **Radiocarbon dating** allows the oldest rocks on Earth to be dated. After certain substances, such as uranium and rubidium, form in rocks, their atoms slowly break down into different atoms. As atoms break down they send out rays, or radioactivity. By assessing how many atoms in a rock have changed, geologists work out the rock's age.

- **Breaks in the sequence** of the geological column are called unconformities.

360 mya

Carboniferous Period: vast warm swamps of fern forests which form coal; first reptiles

408 mya

Devonian Period: first insects and amphibians; ferns and mosses as big as trees

438 mya

Silurian Period: first land plants; fish with jaws and freshwater fish

505 mya

Ordovician Period: early fish-like vertebrates appear; the Sahara is glaciated

590 mya

Cambrian Period: no life on land, but shellfish flourish in the oceans

Precambrian Time: the first life forms (bacteria) appear, and give the air oxygen

7

Shape of the Earth

● **The study of the shape of the Earth** is called geodesy. In the past, geodesy depended on ground-based surveys. Today, satellites play a major role.

● **The Earth is not a perfect sphere**. It is a unique shape called a geoid, which means 'Earth shaped'.

● T**he Earth spins** faster at the Equator than at the Poles, because the Equator is farther from the Earth's spinning axis.

● **The extra speed** of the Earth at the Equator flings it out in a bulge, while it is flattened at the Poles.

▲ *The ancient Greeks realized that the Earth is a globe. Satellite measurements show that it is not quite perfectly round.*

● **Equatorial bulge** was predicted in 1687 by Isaac Newton.

● **The equatorial bulge** was confirmed 70 years after Newton – by French surveys in Peru by Charles de La Condamine, and in Lapland by Pierre de Maupertuis.

- **The Earth's diameter** at the Equator is 12,758 km. This is larger, by 43 km, than the vertical diameter from North Pole to South Pole.

- **The official measurement** of the Earth's radius at the Equator is 6,376,136 m plus or minus 1 m.

- **The Lageos** (Laser Geodynamic) satellite launched in 1976 has measured gravitational differences with extreme precision. It has revealed bumps up to 100 m high, notably just south of India.

- **The Seasat** satellite confirmed the ocean surfaces are geoid. It took millions of measurements of the height of the ocean surface, accurate to within a few centimetres.

Axis

North pole

South pole

▶ The Earth rotates around its axis, the imaginary line running through the centre of the planet from pole to pole at an angle of 23.5°.

The Earth's chemistry

- **The bulk of the Earth** is made from iron, oxygen, magnesium and silicon.

- **More than 80 chemical elements** occur naturally in the Earth and its atmosphere.

- **The crust** is made mostly from oxygen and silicon, with aluminium, iron, calcium, magnesium, sodium, potassium, titanium and traces of 64 other elements.

- **The upper mantle** is made up of iron and magnesium silicates; the lower is silicon and magnesium sulphides and oxides.

- **The core** is mostly iron, with a little nickel and traces of sulphur, carbon, oxygen and potassium.

- **Evidence for the Earth's chemistry** comes from analysing densities with the help of earthquake waves, and from studying stars, meteorites and other planets.

▲ *Zircon crystals found in Australia were 4276 million years old – the oldest part of the Earth's crust ever discovered.*

- **When the Earth** was still semi-molten, dense elements such as iron sank to form the core. Lighter elements such as oxygen floated up to form the crust.

- **Some heavy elements,** such as uranium, ended up in the crust because they easily make compounds with oxygen and silicon.
- **Large blobs of elements** that combine easily with sulphur, such as zinc and lead, spread through the mantle.
- **Elements that combine with iron,** such as gold and nickel, sank to the core.

▼ *This diagram shows the percentages of the chemical elements that make up the Earth.*

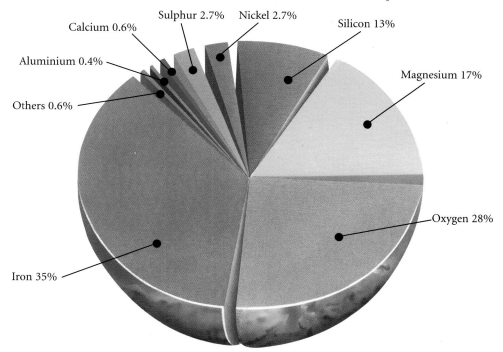

Sulphur 2.7% Nickel 2.7%

Calcium 0.6%

Silicon 13%

Aluminium 0.4%

Others 0.6%

Magnesium 17%

Oxygen 28%

Iron 35%

Earth's interior

- **The Earth's crust** (see crust) is a thin hard outer shell of rock which is a few dozen kilometres thick. Its thickness in relation to the Earth is about the same as the skin on an apple.

- **Under the crust,** there is a deep layer of hot soft rock called the mantle (see core and mantle).

- **The crust and upper mantle** can be divided into three layers according to their rigidity: the lithosphere, the asthenosphere and the mesosphere.

- **Beneath the mantle** is a core of hot iron and nickel. The outer core is so hot – climbing from 4500°C to 6000°C – that it is always molten. The inner core is even hotter (up to 7000°C) but it stays solid because the pressure is 6000 times greater than on the surface.

- **The inner core** contains 1.7% of the Earth's mass, the outer core 30.8%; the core–mantle boundary 3%; the lower mantle 49%; the upper mantle 15%; the ocean crust 0.099% and the continental crust 0.374%.

- **Satellite measurements** are so accurate they can detect slight lumps and dents in the Earth's surface. These indicate where gravity is stronger or weaker because of differences in rock density. Variations in gravity reveal things such as mantle plumes (see hot-spot volcanoes).

▶ *Hot material from the Earth's interior often bursts on to the surface from volcanoes.*

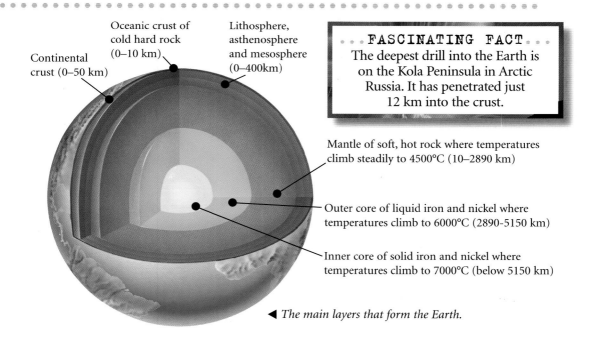

Continental
crust (0–50 km)

Oceanic crust of
cold hard rock
(0–10 km)

Lithosphere,
asthenosphere
and mesosphere
(0–400km)

Mantle of soft, hot rock where temperatures
climb steadily to 4500°C (10–2890 km)

Outer core of liquid iron and nickel where
temperatures climb to 6000°C (2890-5150 km)

Inner core of solid iron and nickel where
temperatures climb to 7000°C (below 5150 km)

◀ *The main layers that form the Earth.*

- **Our knowledge of the Earth's interior** comes mainly from studying how
  earthquake waves move through different kinds of rock.

- **Analysis of how earthquake waves** are deflected reveals where different
  materials occur in the interior. S (secondary) waves pass only through the
  mantle. P (primary) waves pass through the core as well. P waves passing
  through the core are deflected, leaving a shadow zone where no waves reach
  the far side of the Earth.

- **The speed of earthquake waves** reveals how dense the rocky materials are.
  Cold, hard rock transmits waves more quickly than hot, soft rock.

13

The lithosphere

- **The lithosphere** is the upper, rigid layer of the Earth. It consists of the crust and the top of the mantle (see core and mantle). It is about 100 km thick.

- **The lithosphere** was discovered by 'seismology', which means listening to the pattern of vibrations from earthquakes.

- **Fast earthquake waves** show that the top of the mantle is as rigid as the crust, although chemically it is different.

- **Lithosphere** means 'ball of stone'.

- **The lithosphere** is broken into 20 or so slabs, called tectonic plates. The continents sit on top of these plates (see continental drift).

▲ *The hard rocky surface of the Earth is made up of the 20 or so strong rigid plates of the lithosphere.*

- **Temperatures** increase by 35°C for every 1000 m you move down through the lithosphere.

- **Below the lithosphere,** in the Earth's mantle, is the hot, soft rock of the asthenosphere (see Earth's interior).

- **The boundary between the lithosphere** and the asthenosphere occurs at the point where temperatures climb above 1300°C.

- **The lithosphere** is only a few kilometres thick under the middle of the oceans. Here, the mantle's temperature just below the surface is 1300°C.

- **The lithosphere is thickest** – 120 km or so – under the continents.

▲ *The Earth's crust is thin and rocky. All areas of wet and dry land are part of this crust, including the ocean floor.*

Crust

◀ The Earth's crust contains 92 elements.

- **The Earth's crust** is its hard outer shell.

- **The crust** is a thin layer of dense solid rock that floats on the mantle. It is made mainly of silicate minerals (minerals made of silicon and oxygen) such as quartz.

- **There are two kinds of crust:** oceanic and continental.

- **Oceanic crust** is the crust beneath the oceans. It is much thinner – just 7 km thick on average. It is also young, with none being over 200 million years old.

- **Continental crust** is the crust beneath the continents. It is up to 80 km thick and mostly old.

- **Continental crust** is mostly crystalline 'basement' rock up to 3800 million years old. Some geologists think at least half of this rock is over 2500 million years old.

- **It is estimated** that approximately one cubic kilometre of new continental crust is probably being created each year.
- **The 'basement' rock** has two main layers: an upper half of silica-rich rocks such as granite, schist and gneiss, and a lower half of volcanic rocks such as basalt which have less silica. Ocean crust is mostly basalt.
- **Continental crust** is created in the volcanic arcs above subduction zones (see converging plates). Molten rock from the subducted plate oozes to the surface over a period of a few hundred thousand years.
- **The boundary** between the crust and the mantle beneath it is called the Mohorovicic discontinuity.

▶ *The Horn of Africa and the Red Sea is one of the places where the Earth's thin oceanic crust is cracked and moving. It is gradually widening the Red Sea.*

Core and mantle

- **The mantle** makes up the bulk of the Earth's interior. It reaches from about 10–90 km to 2890 km down.

- **As you move** through the mantle temperatures climb steadily, until they reach 3000°C.

- **Mantle rock** is so warm that it churns slowly round like very, very thick treacle boiling on a stove. This movement is known as mantle convection currents.

- **Mantle rock moves** about 10,000 times more slowly than the hour hand on a kitchen clock. Cooler mantle rock takes about 200 million years to sink all the way to the core.

- **Near the surface,** mantle rock may melt into floods of magma. These may gush through the upper layers like oil that is being squeezed from a sponge.

- **The boundary** between the mantle and the core (see Earth's interior) is called the core–mantle boundary (CMB).

- **The CMB** is about 250 km thick. It is an even more dramatic change than between the ground and the air.

- **Temperatures jump by 1500°C** at the CMB.

- **The difference** in density between the core and the mantle at the CMB is twice as great as the difference between air and rock.

▶ *Every now and then, mantle rock melts into floods of magma, which collects along the edges of tectonic plates. It then rises to the surface and erupts as a volcano.*

FASCINATING FACT
Scientists have found 'anti-continents' on the
CMB that match with continents on the surface.

Converging plates

▲ *Volcanoes in subduction zones are usually highly explosive. This is because the magma becomes contaminated as it burns its way up through the continental crust.*

● **In many places** around the world, the tectonic plates that make up the Earth's crust, or outer layer, are slowly crunching together with enormous force.

● **The Atlantic** is getting wider, pushing the Americas further west. Yet the Earth is not getting any bigger because as the American plates crash into the Pacific plates, the thinner, denser ocean plates are driven down into the Earth's hot mantle and are destroyed.

● **The process** of driving an ocean plate down into the Earth's interior is called subduction.

> **FASCINATING FACT**
> Subduction creates a ring of volcanoes around the Pacific Ocean called the 'Ring of Fire'.

● **Subduction** creates deep ocean trenches typically 6–7 km deep at the point of collision. One of these, the Mariana Trench, could drown Mt Everest with 2 km to spare on top.

● **As an ocean plate** bends down into the Earth's mantle, it cracks. The movement of these cracks sets off earthquakes originating up to 700 km down. These earthquake zones are called Benioff–Wadati zones after Hugo Benioff, who discovered them in the 1950s.

● **As an ocean plate** slides down, it melts and makes blobs of magma. This magma floats up towards the surface, punching its way through to create a line of volcanoes along the edge of the continental plate.

- **If volcanoes in subduction zones** emerge in the sea, they form a curving line of volcanic islands called an island arc. Beyond this arc is the back-arc basin, an area of shallow sea that slowly fills up with sediments.

- **As a subducting plate sinks,** the continental plate scrapes sediments off the ocean plate and piles them in a great wedge. Between this wedge and the island arc there may be a fore-arc basin, which is a shallow sea that slowly fills with sediment.

- **Where two continental plates collide,** the plate splits into two layers: a lower layer of dense mantle rock and an upper layer of lighter crustal rock, which is too buoyant to be subducted. As the mantle rock goes down, the crustal rock peels off and crumples against the other to form fold mountains (see mountain ranges).

▼ *This is a cross-section through the top 1000 km or so of the Earth's surface. It shows a subduction zone, where an ocean plate is bent down beneath a continental plate.*

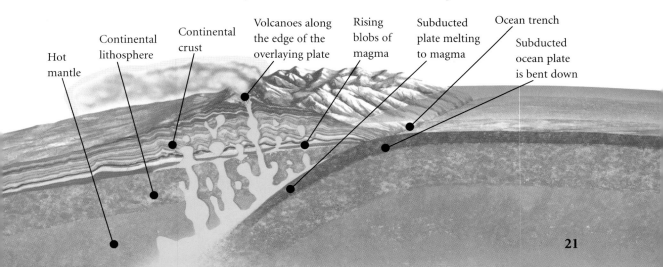

Hot mantle

Continental lithosphere

Continental crust

Volcanoes along the edge of the overlaying plate

Rising blobs of magma

Subducted plate melting to magma

Ocean trench

Subducted ocean plate is bent down

Diverging plates

- **Deep down on the ocean floor,** some of the tectonic plates of the Earth's crust are slowly pushing apart. New molten rock wells up from the mantle into the gap between them and freezes onto their edges. As plates are destroyed at subduction zones, so new plate spreads the ocean floor wider.

- **The spreading of the ocean floor** centres on ridges down the middle of some oceans, mid-ocean ridges. Some of these ridges link up to make the world's longest mountain range, winding over 60,000 km beneath the oceans.

- **The Mid-Atlantic Ridge** stretches through the Atlantic from North Pole to South Pole. The East Pacific Rise winds under the Pacific Ocean from Mexico to Antarctica.

- **Along the middle** of a mid-ocean ridge is a deep canyon. This is where molten rock from the mantle wells up through the sea-bed.

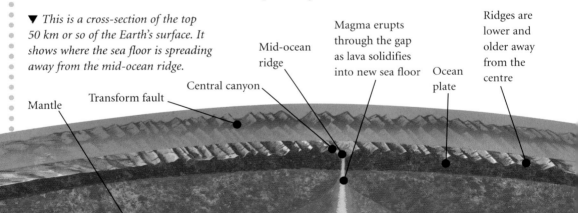

▼ *This is a cross-section of the top 50 km or so of the Earth's surface. It shows where the sea floor is spreading away from the mid-ocean ridge.*

Mid-ocean ridge

Magma erupts through the gap as lava solidifies into new sea floor

Ocean plate

Ridges are lower and older away from the centre

Central canyon

Transform fault

Mantle

- **Mid-ocean ridges** are broken by the curve of the Earth's surface into short stepped sections. Each section is marked off by a long sideways crack called a transform fault. As the sea floor spreads out from a ridge, the sides of the fault rub together setting off earthquakes.

- **As molten rock wells** up from a ridge and freezes, its magnetic material sets in a certain way to line up with the Earth's magnetic field. Because the field reverses every now and then, bands of material set in alternate directions. This means that scientists can see how the sea floor has spread in the past.

▲ *Unlike subduction zones, which create explosive volcanoes, diverging plates create volcanoes that ooze lava gently. For this to happen above the ocean surface is rare.*

- **Rates of sea floor spreading** vary from 1 cm to 20 cm a year. Slow-spreading ridges such as the Mid-Atlantic Ridge are much higher, with seamounts often topping the ridge. Fast-spreading ridges such as the East Pacific Rise are lower, and magma oozes from these just like surface fissure volcanoes.

- **Hot magma** bubbling up through a mid-ocean ridge emerges as hot lava. As it comes into contact with the cold seawater it freezes into blobs, pillow lava.

- **Mid-ocean ridges** may begin where a mantle plume (see hot-spot volcanoes) rises through the mantle and melts through the sea-bed.

⸱⸱⸱**FASCINATING FACT**⸱⸱⸱
About 10 cubic km of new crust is created at the mid-ocean ridges every year.

Tectonic plates

- **The Earth's surface** is divided into slabs called tectonic plates. Each plate is a fragment of the Earth's rigid outer layer, or lithosphere (see the lithosphere).

- **There are 16 large plates** and several smaller ones. Plates are approximately 100 km thick but can vary in thickness from 8 km to 200 km.

- **The biggest plate** is the Pacific plate, which underlies the whole of the Pacific Ocean. The Pacific Ocean represents half of the world's ocean area.

- **Tectonic plates** are moving all the time – by about 10 cm a year. Over hundreds of millions of years they move vast distances. Some have moved halfway round the globe.

- **The continents** are embedded in the tops of the plates, so as the plates move the continents move with them.

- **The Pacific plate** is the only large plate with no part of a continent situated on it. It represents more than one-third of the Earth's surface area.

- **The movement** of tectonic plates accounts for many things, including the pattern of volcanic and earthquake activity around the world.

▲ *Beneath the Pacific Ocean lies the Pacific plate, the largest of the tectonic plates.*

- **There are three kinds** of boundary between plates: convergent, divergent and transform.

- **Tectonic plates** are probably driven by convection currents of molten rock that circulate within the Earth's mantle (see core and mantle).

- **The lithosphere** was too thin for tectonic plates until 500 million years ago.

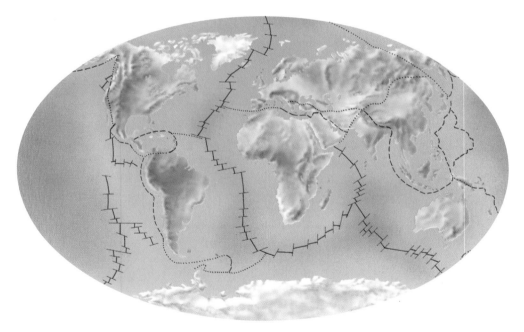

▲ *This map shows some of the jagged boundaries between plates.*

Volcanoes

- **Volcanoes** are places where magma (red-hot liquid rock from the Earth's interior) emerges through the crust and onto the surface.

- **The word 'volcano'** comes from Vulcano Island in the Mediterranean. Here Vulcan, the ancient Roman god of fire and blacksmith to the gods, was supposed to have forged his weapons in the fire beneath the mountain.

- **There are many types** of volcano (see kinds of volcano). The most distinctive are the cone-shaped composite volcanoes, which build up from alternating layers of ash and lava in successive eruptions.

- **Beneath a composite volcano** there is typically a large reservoir of magma called a magma chamber. Magma collects in the chamber before an eruption.

- **From the magma chamber** a narrow chimney, or vent, leads up to the surface. It passes through the cone of debris from previous eruptions.

- **When a volcano erupts,** the magma is driven up the vent by the gases within it. As the magma nears the surface, the pressure drops, allowing the gases dissolved in the magma to boil out. The expanding gases – mostly carbon dioxide and steam – push the molten rock upwards and out of the vent.

> ...**FASCINATING FACT**...
> At Urgüp, Turkey, volcanic ash has been blown into tall cones by gas fumes bubbling up. The cones have hardened like huge salt cellars. People have dug them out to make homes.

- **If the level of magma** in the magma chamber drops, the top of the volcano's cone may collapse into it, forming a giant crater called a caldera. Caldera is Spanish for 'boiling pot'. The world's largest caldera is Toba on Sumatra, Indonesia, which is 1775 sq km.

- **When a volcano** with a caldera subsides, the whole cone may collapse into the old magma chamber. The caldera may fill with water to form a crater lake, such as Crater Lake in Oregon, USA.

- **All the magma** does not gush up the central vent. Some exits through branching side vents, often forming their own small 'parasitic' cones on the side of the main one.

Volcanic bombs, or tephra, are fragments of the shattered volcanic plug flung out far and wide

Before each eruption, the vent is clogged by old volcanic material from previous eruptions. The explosion blows the plug into tiny pieces of ash and cinder, and blasts them high into the air

Central vent

Side vent

Magma chamber where magma collects before an eruption

Earthquakes

- **Earthquakes** are a shaking of the ground. Some are slight tremors that barely rock a cradle. Others are so violent they can tear down mountains.

- **Small earthquakes** may be set off by landslides, volcanoes or even just heavy traffic. Big earthquakes are set off by the grinding together of the vast tectonic plates that make up the Earth's surface.

- **Tectonic plates** are sliding past each other all the time, but sometimes they stick. The rock bends and stretches for a while and then snaps. This makes the plates jolt, sending out the shock waves that cause the earthquake's effects to be felt far away.

- **Tectonic plates** typically slide 4 or 5 cm past each other in a year. In a slip that triggers a major quake they can slip more than 1 m in a few seconds.

- **In most quakes** a few minor tremors (foreshocks) are followed by an intense burst lasting just one or two minutes. A second series of minor tremors (aftershocks) occurs over the next few hours.

- **The starting point** of an earthquake below ground is called the hypocentre, or focus. The epicentre of an earthquake is the point on the surface directly above the hypocentre.

- **Earthquakes are strongest** at the epicentre and become gradually weaker farther away.

- **Certain regions** called earthquake zones are especially prone to earthquakes. Earthquake zones lie along the edges of tectonic plates.

- **A shallow earthquake** originates 0–70 km below the ground. These are the ones that do the most damage. An intermediate quake begins 70–300 km down. Deep quakes begin over 300 km down. The deepest-ever recorded earthquake began over 720 km down.

▼ *During an earthquake, shock waves radiate in circles outwards and upwards from the focus of the earthquake. The damage caused is greatest at the epicentre, where the waves are strongest, but vibrations may be felt 400 km away.*

··· FASCINATING FACT ···
The longest recorded earthquake, in Alaska on March 21, 1964, lasted just four minutes.

As two tectonic plates jolt past each other, they send out shock waves

Isoseismic lines show where the quake's intensity is equal

The quake's intensity is reduced away from the epicentre

Epicentre

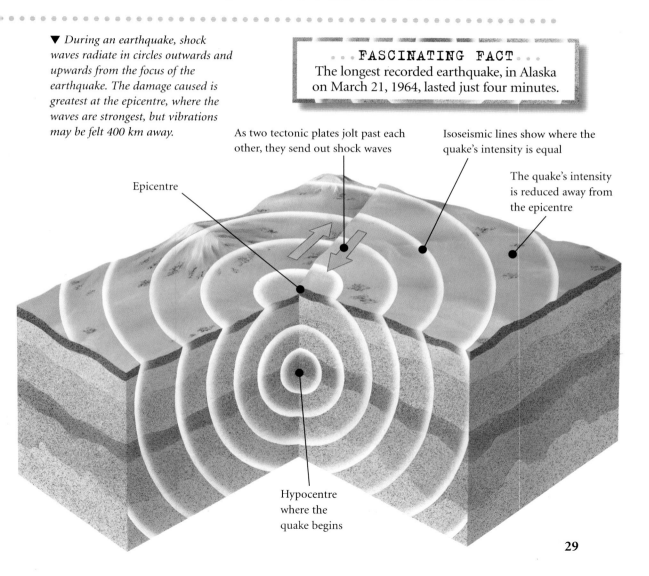

Hypocentre where the quake begins

29

Faults

- **A fault** is a fracture in rock along which large blocks of rock have slipped past each other.

- **Faults usually occur** in fault zones, which are often along the boundaries between tectonic plates. Faults are typically caused by earthquakes.

- **Single earthquakes** rarely move blocks more than a few centimetres. Repeated small earthquakes can shift blocks hundreds of kilometres.

- **Compression faults** are faults caused by rocks being squeezed together, perhaps by converging plates.

- **Tension faults** are faults caused by rocks being pulled together, perhaps by diverging plates.

- **Normal, or dip-slip, faults** are tension faults where the rock fractures and slips straight down.

▲ *Unlike most faults the San Andreas Fault in California is visible on the Earth's surface.*

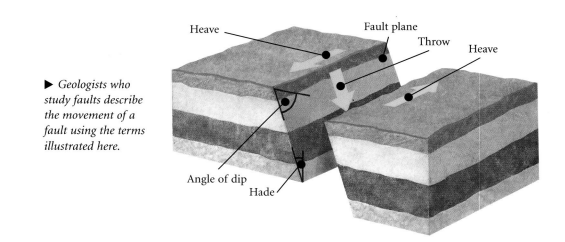

Heave   Fault plane   Throw   Heave

▶ Geologists who study faults describe the movement of a fault using the terms illustrated here.

Angle of dip   Hade

- **A wrench, or tear, fault** occurs when plates slide past each other and make blocks slip horizontally.

- **Large wrench faults,** such as the San Andreas in California, USA, are called transcurrent faults.

- **Rift valleys** are huge, trough-shaped valleys created by faulting, such as Africa's Great Rift Valley. The floor is a thrown-down block called a graben. Some geologists think they are caused by tension, others by compression.

- **Horst blocks** are blocks of rock thrown up between normal faults, often creating a high plateau.

Folds

- **Rocks usually form** in flat layers called strata. Tectonic plates can collide (see converging plates) with such force that they crumple up these strata.

- **Sometimes the folds** are just tiny wrinkles a few centimetres long. Sometimes they are gigantic, with hundreds of kilometres between crests (the highest points on a fold).

- **The shape of a fold** depends on the force that is squeezing it and on the resistance of the rock.

- **The slope of a fold** is called the dip. The direction of the dip is the direction in which it is sloping.

- **The strike of the fold** is at right angles to the dip. It is the horizontal alignment of the fold.

- **Some folds turn right over** on themselves to form upturned folds called nappes.

◀ *The Alps in Europe are fold mountains. They formed when two of the Earth's plates collided. This collision caused layers of rocks to crumple and fold.*

- **As nappes fold on top of other nappes,** the crumpled strata may pile up into mountains.

- **A downfold** is called a syncline; an upfolded arch of strata is called an anticline.

- **The axial plane** of a fold divides the fold into halves.

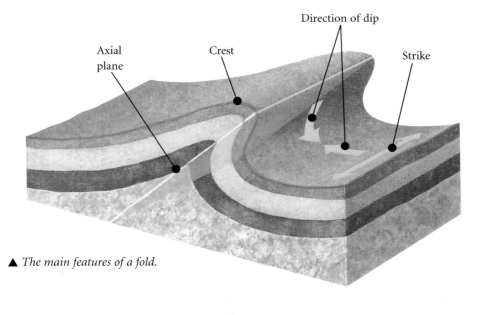

▲ *The main features of a fold.*

······**FASCINATING FACT**····
Most of the world's oil comes from
reservoirs that are trapped in anticlines.

Rocks

▲ *The Kent coast near Dover is famous for its white cliffs which are made of chalk.*

- **The oldest known rocks** on Earth are 3900 million years old – they are the Acasta gneiss rocks from Canada.

- **There are three main kinds of rock:** igneous rock, sedimentary rock and metamorphic rock.

- **Igneous rocks** (igneous means 'fiery') are made when hot molten magma or lava cools and solidifies.

- **Volcanic rocks,** such as basalt, are igneous rocks that form from lava that has erupted from volcanoes.

- **Metamorphic rocks** are rocks that have changed over time, such as limestone which is made into marble because of the heat generated by magma.

- **Sedimentary rocks** are rocks that are made from the slow hardening of sediments into layers, or strata.

- **Some sedimentary rocks,** such as sandstone, are made from sand and silt. Other rocks are broken down into these materials by weathering and erosion.

- **Most sediments** form on the sea-bed. Sand is washed down onto the sea-bed by rivers.

- **Limestone and chalk** are sedimentary rocks made mainly from the remains of sea creatures.

▶ *Rocks are continually recycled. Whether they form from volcanoes or sediments, all rocks are broken down into sand by weathering and erosion. The sand is deposited on sea-beds and river-beds where it hardens to form new rock. This process is the rock cycle.*

Fossils

▼ *Scientists study fossils to learn about the Earth's history and about the animals and plants that lived millions of years ago.*

- **Fossils** are the remains of living things preserved for millions of years, usually in stone.

- **Most fossils** are the remains of living things such as bones, shells, eggs, leaves and seeds.

- **Trace fossils** are fossils of signs left behind by creatures, such as footprints and scratch marks.

- **Paleontologists** (scientists who study fossils) tell the age of a fossil from the rock layer in which it is found. Also, they measure how the rock has changed radioactively since it was formed (radiocarbon dating).

- **The oldest fossils** are called stromatolites. They are fossils of big, pizza-like colonies of microscopic bacteria over 3500 million years old.

36

▶ *When an animal dies, its soft parts rot away quickly. If its bones or shell are buried quickly in mud, they may turn to stone. When a shellfish such as this ancient trilobite dies and sinks to the sea-bed, its shell is buried. Over millions of years, water trickling through the mud may dissolve the shell, but minerals in the water fill its place to make a perfect cast.*

- **The biggest fossils** are conyphytons, 2000-million-year-old stromatolites over 100 m high.

- **Not all fossils** are stone. Mammoths have been preserved by being frozen in the permafrost (see cold landscapes) of Siberia.

- **Insects** have been preserved in amber, the solidified sap of ancient trees.

- **Certain widespread, short-lived fossils** are very useful for dating rock layers. These are known as index fossils.

- **Index fossils** include ancient shellfish such as trilobites, graptolites, crinoids, belemnites, ammonites and brachiopods.

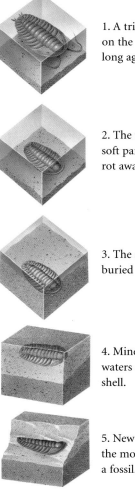

1. A trilobite dies on the ocean floor long ago.

2. The trilobite's soft parts eventually rot away.

3. The shell is slowly buried by mud.

4. Mineral-rich waters dissolve the shell.

5. New minerals fill the mould to form a fossil.

37

Gems and crystals

- **Gems** are mineral crystals that are beautifully coloured or sparkling.

- **There are over 3000 minerals** but only 130 are gemstones. Only about 50 of these are commonly used.

- **The rarest gems** are called precious gems and include diamonds, emeralds and rubies.

- **Less rare gems** are known as semi-precious gems.

- **Gems** are weighed in carats. A carat is one-fifth of a gram. A 50-carat sapphire is very large and very valuable.

- **In the ancient world** gems were weighed with carob seeds. The word 'carat' comes from the Arabic for seed.

▲ *Many minerals are made as magma cools. When this happens crystals, such as amethyst crystals, are formed.*

▶ *There are more than 100
different kinds of gemstone.*

Diamond

Garnet

Topaz

Emerald

- **Gems** often form in gas bubbles called geodes in
  cooling magma. They can also form when hot magma
  packed with minerals seeps up through cracks in the
  rock to form a vein.

- **When magma** cools, minerals with the highest melting
  points crystallize first. Unusual minerals are left
  behind to crystallize last, forming rocks called
  pegmatites. These rocks are often rich in gems such as
  emeralds, garnets, topazes and tourmalines.

- **Some gems** with a high melting point and simple
  chemical composition form directly from magma,
  such as diamond, which is pure carbon, and rubies.

... **FASCINATING FACT** ...
Diamonds are among the oldest mineral
crystals, over 3000 million years old.

39

Index